Acknowledgements

The Open Spaces Society wishes to record its heartfelt thanks to the helped with the research, drafting, checking, typing, re-typing publishing. It would be difficult to name everyone, but they include:

David Ainger, Kate Ashbrook, Nicole Bentham, Paul Clayden, Pat Folland, Richard Harland, David Jefferson, Julie Jiggens, Paul Johnson, George Laurence QC, Jerry Pearlman, Edgar Powell, Inge Robinson, Gerard Ryan QC, Alec Samuels, Roger Sims, Hilary Woodward, and all who spoke at and contributed to our two seminars on registering new greens in November 1994.

The front-cover picture, of children at Low Bradfield near Sheffield, was photographed by Simon Warner.

The drawings are by Emma Whiting.

Thanks

We are most grateful to the Countryside Commission for grant-aiding this manual and the two seminars which fed into it.

In particular, we thank Paul Johnson for his help and support.

We also wish warmly to acknowledge donations from the Frognal Trust and the Norman Franklin Charitable Trust.

Published by The Open Spaces Society, 25A Bell Street, Henley-on-Thames, Oxon RG9 2BA

Typeset *(in Monotype Baskerville)* and printed by Powage Press, Aspley Guise, Milton Keynes MK17 8HF

Foreword

The traditional village green is a place to treasure. It is likely to have been the setting for events, announcements and gatherings of historical interest. Generations of local people will have used it for recreations which we may now be pleased to call 'customary' but many of which – not all perhaps – will have come and gone. The green may also lie at a central or critical location in the town or the village and contribute, in the fashionable phrase, to the 'sense of place'.

In 1965 the Commons Registration Act caught town greens and village greens within the net of registration. Many were properly registered, though some were missed and others wrongly registered. That all happened several decades ago. Today, any land which is not already registered and 'on which the inhabitants of any locality have indulged in lawful sports and pastimes, as of right, for not less than 20 years' is eligible to be registered as a 'new' green under the Commons Registration (New Land) Regulations 1969. This manual clearly explains the meaning and significance of the various statutory requirements and the procedure to be followed in order to achieve registration. It is worth remembering that the registration of land as a green may often, though not always, generate protection against development in a town planning context.

Reports and papers are regularly described as 'essential reading'. For anyone setting out to register a village green or town green this manual genuinely is essential reading. It is, I believe, the only comprehensive publication on the subject: it is certainly indispensable in understanding it. The manual has been compiled with much care and with a due sense of caution when discussing matters that remain undecided by the courts. Here is a commentary in plain English on each topic that needs consideration in an overall appreciation of the issues that are likely to arise. While being the obvious guide for all whose prior knowledge of the subject may be rather hazy, this manual is also likely to be of value to commons registration authorities, and to their advisers, in reaching decisions about registration.

The status of land as a green raises some issues that are still not finally resolved as questions of law. It follows that not all lawyers will agree with every word of this manual. I do not think this matters, nor is it a criticism of the approach to the subject adopted by the Open Spaces Society. A notable characteristic of its manual is the impartiality of its approach. I suspect that it is likely to prove as valuable to those who oppose claims as to those who initiate them! The Society is to be congratulated on its success in bringing together all the features of this fascinating subject in a user-friendly way. I enthusiastically commend the result.

Gerard Ryan QC

Contents

Appendices

1. The Commons Registration (New Land) Regulations 1969, SI 1843, Form 30, statutory declaration form and notes

2. Lawful sports and pastimes

3. Evidence questionnaire in support of claim for registration as a new green

4. Likely sequence of events in registering new greens

5. Inclosure Act 1857 section 12 and Commons Act 1876 section 29

6. Scope for reform of the law on town and village greens

7. Bibliography

Introduction

This manual explains the procedure for registering town or village greens, and considers in detail the key legal principles which govern this area of law.

It comprehensively replaces and updates the guidance on the registration of greens given in the Society's book *Our Common Land* and information sheets. It features important changes, based on cases decided and counsel's opinions received since the earlier guidance was compiled. This is by far the most detailed advice ever to be published for registration authorities and applicants on this complex subject.

The Society would very much like to hear of cases with which readers of this manual become involved, so that future editions can properly reflect emerging law and practice in this area.

Town or village green

1. Story-book images of greens tend to be of an area of grass in the centre of a village complete with oak tree and seat, or a carefully-manicured recreation ground just outside with its own cricket pitch and pavilion.

2. In legal terms, the expression 'town or village green' has a much wider meaning. It has long been used to describe any area of land, rural or urban, over which the inhabitants of a particular locality hold customary recreational rights. The courts have formally recognised such customs as good in law since at least the seventeenth century. Nineteenth-century legislation made it an offence to encroach on or inclose town or village greens, or to interfere with local people's use of them.

3. The Commons Registration Act 1965 ('the 1965 Act') set up official registers of commons and of town and village greens. The initial registration period ran between 1967 and 1970. Applications to register commons and greens were invited from any person, whether that person had any legal interest in the land or not. All the land applied for was compiled into a set of provisional registers for each county. Disputed cases were decided upon by specially-appointed Commons Commissioners. Land remaining on the register then became 'finally' registered. A final registration represents conclusive legal evidence that the land was common land or a town or village green, as the case may be, at the date of registration.

4. In providing for the registration of greens, the Act offered the first ever statutory definition:

   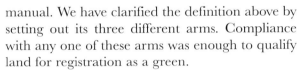

   > **'Town or village green' means land –**
   >
   > • **which has been allotted by or under any Act for the exercise or recreation of the inhabitants of any locality; or**
   >
   > • **on which the inhabitants of any locality have a customary right to indulge in lawful sports and pastimes; or**
   >
   > • **on which the inhabitants of any locality have indulged in such sports and pastimes, as of right, for not less than 20 years.**

5. This definition appears in section 22(1) of the 1965 Act. We refer to it a good deal in this manual. We have clarified the definition above by setting out its three different arms. Compliance with any one of these arms was enough to qualify land for registration as a green.

6. The original registration exercise closed on 31 July 1970. Land which was not on the registers at that date was not thereafter recognised by the 1965 Act as a common or a green. The effect of this sanction is considered later.

7. Section 13(b) of the 1965 Act, and regulations made under it, provide for the greens registers to be amended to include any land which becomes a town or village green after July 1970. The word 'becomes' is somewhat confusing here. Situations do arise where land genuinely starts being used as a green for the first time, having had no previous use as such. But most examples of greens registration concern areas of land which have a long history of recreational use by local inhabitants. They only 'become' greens in the sense of becoming legally recognised by the 1965 Act, having not been recognised by the Act as greens for the period since the registers closed on 31 July 1970.

8. This 'becoming' a green requires some kind of 'event' after July 1970 which has the effect of making the land recognisable once more by the 1965 Act. The event upon which most new registrations rely is the passing of at least 20 years during which the local inhabitants have used the land for lawful sports and pastimes, as of right. By

such use, the land achieves compliance with the third arm of the greens definition reproduced above, and so 'becomes ... a town or village green' for the purposes of the 1965 Act.

9. As under the original registration exercise, any person may apply for registration of a town or village green, using the special form described later. Application is made to the registration authority, which (subject to any impact of local government reorganisation) is the county council, London borough or metropolitan council in question. The procedure is set out by the Commons Registration (New Land) Regulations 1969, SI 1843 ('the Regulations'). These were published by Her Majesty's Stationery Office, but are out of print. The relevant regulations, including application forms and notes, are reproduced in Appendix 1.

10. Although any person may apply, the case for registration must be properly considered and assembled in accordance with the guidance below. There is however no provision for costs to be awarded against an applicant who puts forward an ill-founded case for registration. Under the original registration procedure, Commons Commissioners had power under section 17(4) of the 1965 Act to award costs in appropriate circumstances; but registration authorities, who must decide upon new applications for registration, have no comparable powers.

11. In view of the emphasis placed by most new applications on the third arm of the greens definition which is reproduced in paragraph 4 above, the various components of this third arm are now considered.

Land . . . on which

12. When the 1965 Act speaks of 'land ... on which' local inhabitants have indulged in lawful sports and pastimes, it means just that. Their use must relate to an area of land, rather than simply to one or more routes through it from A to B.

13. Accidental wandering off the line of a public right of way will therefore not justify registration as a green. But the presence of rights of way need not inhibit an application for registration as a green, so long as it is clear that the inhabitants' recreational use (as opposed to their passage from A to B) is genuinely not confined to specific routes over the land.

14. The area of land on which the lawful sports and pastimes take place needs to be identified with care, and clearly defined

on a map. This is required by statutory application Form 30, attached to the Regulations.

15. The applicant must show with some certainty that lawful sports and pastimes have taken place over the land. It may be that different parts of the land will have been used for different recreational purposes. That does not matter, but area-wide use of the land by local inhabitants for recreational purposes must be clear.

16. The registrable area includes surrounding land which can fairly be regarded as part of the same piece of land which has been used for lawful sports and pastimes. So long as the land is well defined, it will not be necessary to show that every last part of it has been used in this way.[1] But the more extensive the site, and the less clear its boundaries, the more a detailed correlation between type and location of recreational use is likely to be required.

17. It may not be possible to get to all of the land all of the time. For example, parts may be dense undergrowth, blackberry bushes, wild roses; parts may be swampy, especially in wet weather, making those parts either unusable or only usable to a

---

(1) See the Commons Commissioner's decision *re land at Byfield, Northamptonshire* (1972) 26/D 19-21. Individual decisions of the Commons Commissioners are available from their offices at Golden Cross House, Duncannon Street, London WC2N 4JF (0171 210 4584).

limited extent. So long as these clearly form part of the whole single unit of land, they are registrable.[1]

18. Parts may be temporarily inaccessible because the owner, such as a local authority, is engaged in such works of improvement or maintenance as earth-moving, earth-levelling, draining, soil-laying, coppicing, grass cutting or planting. Again, this will not affect the registrability.

19. Controlled tipping by or with the consent of the local authority, might be small-scale, part of an improvement scheme, and not such as substantially to interfere with the sports and pastimes; but if it has been the major use of the land over the period to which the claim refers, it is unlikely to have been compatible with the use of the land for lawful sports and pastimes.[2]

The inhabitants of any locality

20. If most recreational use of the land is by the general public, then it is too wide to justify registration as a green. Recreational use must be only or mainly by the *inhabitants of a defined locality* if it is to support registration.

21. It would of course be wrong if, for example, the fact that a public right of way crosses land, or that periodic events such as fêtes which attract visitors from further afield, were to disqualify an application for registration.

22. Equally, it would seem unreasonable for even substantial use of a green by the employees of local factories or offices to prejudice a claim for registration, simply because many of the workers travel daily from the surrounding area. So long as the locality cited on the application includes any local workplaces from which significant amounts of recreational use of the green emanate, it seems reasonable to regard their employees not simply as parts of the community but as inhabitants of the locality, for the purposes of the application. This is not however a point which has been tested in court, to the Society's knowledge.

23. If a major proportion of the recreational use which takes place over the land in question involves people who neither live nor have their workplace in the defined locality, then the case for registration is likely to fail, because the claim is too wide to be recognised by the law of greens. This need not rule out asking a court to recognise a different type of recreational right in such a case, eg under charity law.[3]

24. It may be that an application will use the term 'the public' loosely, meaning people from the community as distinct from those with legal interests in the land. Although this is potentially confusing, it should not of itself invalidate the application so long as it is clear from the evidence that the use is primarily by local inhabitants rather than the general public.

25. The town or village green itself need not form part of the geographical locality which it serves, nor immediately adjoin it. But the further away it is, the better the evidence needed to establish town or village green status.

26. The key locality tests are therefore:

- *is there a particular and recognisable community or neighbourhood where most of the recreational users of the land live or work?*
- *can the boundaries of this locality be clearly shown on a map?*
- *is the locality sufficiently near the land itself to establish a clear link with it?*

27. The defined locality need not equate to any recognised administrative boundaries – but it may do so. It may for example be a parish[4] (and often was in nineteenth-century cases), or a village,[5] or even a town.[6]

28. The locality may also be two or more parishes. *Edwards* v *Jenkins*[7] ruled against this, but the correctness of this ruling was doubted by the Court of Appeal in *New Windsor Corporation* v *Mellor*.[8]

29. Subject to the requirement of identification, clear boundaries and map delineation, a neighbourhood or a community or housing estate may qualify.[9] But locality cannot be defined only by reference to persons – it must be defined by reference to geography.

30. Too strict a requirement for definition of the relevant locality would defeat most applications, particularly in urban areas. Counsel has advised that registration authorities need to take a common-sense approach where there are definitional problems.

31. A local survey can help to establish the true pattern of use. A survey of actual users of the land, on the spot, may yield more accurate information

(1) See for example *Lancashire* v *Hunt* (1894) 10 TLR 310 and the Commons Commissioner case of *Gleaston Green, Aldingham, Lancashire* (1972) 20/D/3.
(2) Report on *Peartree Green, Southampton, Hampshire* (1992) by Vivian Chapman of counsel. Report on *Post Hill Quarries, Leeds, West Yorkshire* (1988) by Charles George of counsel.
(3) See for example *R* v *Doncaster Metropolitan Council ex parte Braim* (1987) 85 LGR 233. *Peggs* v *Lamb* (1994) 2 WLR 1, Morritt J. *Making Space* (1992), chapter 24.
(4) *Forbes* v *Ecclesiastical Commissioners for England* (1872) LR 15 Eq 51.
(5) *Lancashire* v *Hunt* (1894) 10 TLR 310.
(6) *Mounsey* v *Ismay* (1863) 1 H and C 729, 734, Pollock CB.
(7) *Edwards* v *Jenkins* (1896) 1 Ch 308, Kekewich J.
(8) *New Windsor Corporation* v *Mellor* (1975) 1 Ch 380, 387 Denning MR 396 Brightman LJ.
(9) See for example the Commons Commissioner case of *Silverhill Park Pleasure Ground, St Leonards-on-Sea, East Sussex* (1979) 83/D/1.

as to the true nature of the locality which it serves (and the balance with any 'public' use) than would a house-to-house survey of a particular area which is assumed to be the locality.

32. A house-to-house survey may nevertheless yield useful information. But intending applicants should first gather together all the information and then, and only then, should the claimed locality be identified if it looks appropriate to proceed with an application.

Lawful sports and pastimes

33. *'There are certain rights which may be claimed by custom, as distinct from prescription. What is called a right of recreation and amusement, of air and exercise, or the playing of all manner of lawful games and pastimes, is a right in the nature of an easement which may be well claimed by custom.'*[1]

34. Sir George Jessel's remarks form part of a remarkably lucid judgment on the whole subject of customary recreational rights for the inhabitants of a locality. They reinforce the fact that a very wide range of activities can be, and have been, recognised under the local law of custom, as distinct from the general common law.

35. Despite the breadth of Sir George Jessel's summary of the law, some modern commentators have pointed to the fact that the first arm of the greens definition uses different terminology from the second and third as evidence that Parliament intended to exclude simple exercise and recreation from the scope of 'lawful sports and pastimes'. In fact, both counsel and Commons Commissioners[2] have taken the view that 'lawful sports and pastimes' include exercise and recreation, as well as organised games. Community events such as fêtes, maypole celebrations, flower shows or carol singing on the green are also lawful pastimes.

36. Isolated individual use will not be enough to support registration, unless separate instances of it add up to form an overall picture of community use. For example, the fact that one person walks on the land or flies a kite there would not form any basis for registration. But if a variety of people from the local community use the land for walking or for flying kites, albeit in a solitary way, the overall pattern could be one of qualifying use.

37. It is sometimes wrongly stated that the famous case of *AG* v *Antrobus*[3] – the Stonehenge case – ruled that the right to wander around land was unknown to the law. In fact, the Antrobus decision concerned the law of grant or prescription, and counsel has advised that it does not prevent

recreational walking over areas of land from forming part of the lawful sports and pastimes on which a claim for registration of land as a green is based.

38. The activities specified in an application for registration must be certain, ie capable of definition, and there must be clear evidence that they actually take place on the land. The fact that the land has other established uses (such as grazing stock or growing hay) need not call into question a claim for registration as a green, so long as the lawful sports and pastimes specified on the application actually take place too, at the times and in the ways stated.

39. Civil law considerations, such as the fact that local people may be felt to be trespassing in the absence of any recognised right, or the fact that their activities may cause some degree of nuisance or incidental disruption to land management or to adjoining residents, do not take activities outside the scope of 'lawful sports and pastimes'. 'Lawful' simply excludes activities which break the

(1) Jessel MR, *Hammerton* v *Honey* (1876) 24 WR 603
(2) See for example the Commons Commissioner case of *Silverhill Park Pleasure Ground, St Leonards-on-Sea, East Sussex* (1979) 83/D/1.
(3) *Attorney-General* v *Antrobus* (1905) 2 Ch 188, 198-199, 207.

criminal law, such as prize fighting, cock fighting or bull baiting.

40. There are numerous judicial and Commons Commissioner decisions on whether specified activities do in fact constitute lawful sports and pastimes. Each case turns on its own particular facts, and on the cumulative effect of the activities. Appendix 2 lists some of the specific activities which have been recognised by the courts or the commissioners as relevant for this purpose.

41. Commercial activities such as drying fishing nets, selling goods, commercial fairs or fruit picking for sale, do not qualify as lawful sports and pastimes. Nor does car parking.

As of right

42. Where an application to register land as a green relies on 20 years' use by local inhabitants, it can only succeed if this use was 'as of right'.

43. This means that the use must have taken place without force, without stealth or secrecy, and without permission – or, in the Latin phrase, '*nec vi, nec clam, nec precario*'.

Without force

44. If at any point during the 20-year period on which the claim depends, people had to force their way onto the land in order to pursue their 'lawful sports and pastimes', this would rule out a claim that their use was as of right. Once 20 years of qualifying use without force has elapsed, however, any reasonable force which subsequently has to be used in order to remove new obstructions to local people's use would not rule out a claim, if it was otherwise well founded. It is important for a claim to be pursued promptly once any resistance to recreational use has begun.

Without stealth or secrecy

45. If people have only gone onto the land at night, or at other times when they know that the owner and his agents are unlikely to be present, it would be difficult to claim that their use was 'as of right'. But if a landowner has simply been unaware that people were using the land for lawful sports and pastimes, for example because he lives elsewhere, this would not weaken the claim.

Without permission

46. If interpreted too broadly, the requirement for use to be 'without permission' might alone rule out most claims to register greens. A claim by the landowner that he simply *tolerated* use by local inhabitants, for example, might be taken to defeat an application. Some court judgments in relation to prescriptive claims (a different area of law) do accept tolerance as the sole basis of long use.[1] Others have ruled that only express permission and acceptance of such permission, from time to time during the claim period, defeat a claim that use was 'without permission', and therefore as of right.[2]

47. The matter is further complicated by the fact that if local people have been using land as of right for many years, even the formal grant, late in the day, of permission to use the land will not nullify a claim, so long as the period to which the claim refers was not itself covered by such permission. Equally, the fact that the owner may have given formal permission for certain specific use of the land (for example by a visiting angling club or football club for regular matches) need not invalidate a claim that the local inhabitants used the land as of right for lawful sports and pastimes.

48. The best way to make the 'without permission' judgment seems to be to consider whether, on all the facts, the use by local inhabitants that actually took place during the claim period appears to have originated from, or relied upon, permission or tolerance by the owner – or whether no such permission or tolerance was sought or, even if it was sought, was needed. The fact that the owner did nothing to prevent or discourage use for lawful sports and pastimes over the claim period may simply confirm that use was as of right.[3]

49. It is not essential for users to *believe* they have any legal right to use the land in the way they do, so

---

(1) See for example *Alfred F Beckett Ltd* v *Lyons* (1967) Ch 449.
(2) See for example *Earl de la Warr* v *Miles* (1881) 17 Ch D at 596. The Commons Commissioner's decision *re Rodmersham Green, Kent* (1976) 219/D/19-22 features a long discussion of permission and tolerance.
(3) The Commons Commissioner's decision *re Rodmersham Green, Kent* (1976) 219/D/19-22 contains a long discussion of the difference between real permission, formal permission and tolerance in this context.

long as by their conduct they have shown that they use the land without force, secrecy or permission.[1]

50. Use of land by local inhabitants under an actual legal right such as a customary recreational right or an express or inferred charitable trust counts as use 'as of right' for the purposes of section 22(1).[2] Regulation of lawful sports and pastimes by a committee does not negate a claim that use was 'as of right'.[3]

51. When analysing whether use is without permission, exactly the same tests should be applied to land owned or held on trust by a local authority, or other public-sector body, as to privately-owned land. The judgment must be on the facts of the particular case.[4]

52. Can children go on land 'as of right'? The argument for accepting that they can is that they thought they could use a piece of land, they did so, and no one ever stopped them. The argument against is that they are too young to think about or to understand jurisprudential theory and legal right: they simply trespassed on land to play, as children do. Usually there is evidence of other sports and pastimes too, so that children playing is not normally considered in isolation, but may form part of the overall picture of use. Appendix 2 lists some relevant cases.

53. The persistence of a place-name in the form 'X Green' will strengthen a claim that land, particularly uncultivated land, is subject to customary recreational rights for local inhabitants, so long as the other evidence is consistent with such a finding.[5] The possible existence of such customary rights will support rather than inhibit a claim that 20 years' user has been 'as of right'.

Not less than 20 years

54. It was stated earlier that to justify registration, it is necessary to show that something has occurred since the original registration exercise finished in 1970, by which land has 'become' a green for the purposes of the Act. The something usually relied on for this purpose is the expiry of an identifiable period of not less than 20 years during which qualifying use by local people has taken place, thus bringing the land within the third arm of the greens definition (reproduced at paragraph 4).

Continuity

55. The period of use referred to in the application must have been continuous. This does not mean that the land must have been used for lawful sports and pastimes on every day or every week or month of the 20 years (or longer) which ended on the date stated. But if it is proved that there has been a substantial period of interruption during the period cited, during which local inhabitants' use was effectively resisted or withdrawn, then the claim will not be good. Only a further 20-year period of use, subsequent to the interruption, will then satisfy the requirement.

56. Once there has been 20 years' continuous use, subsequent interruption will not be fatal to the claim. But, as explained below, interruption does emphasise the need to pursue the claim without unnecessary delay, in order to maintain its credibility.

57. There is no implication that the same activities must have been carried on for the whole of the period specified. What is required is that, during the period, an adequate level of lawful sports and pastimes took place on the land to justify the claim. That the activities may have varied seasonally or over time is of no consequence, so long as the overall pattern is one of qualifying use.

(1) Report on land at Emmet's Park, Binfield, Berkshire (1994) by Vivian Chapman of counsel.
(2) The Commons Commissioner's decision re Gleaston Green, Aldingham, Lancashire (1972) 20/D/3, and re The Village Green, Abthorpe, Northamptonshire (1979) 226/D/40-54.
(3) re Gleaston Green, Aldingham, Lancashire (1972)   20/D/3.
(4) See for example the Commons Commissioner's decision re Fordington Green, Dorchester, Dorset (1973) 10/D/17.
(5) The Commons Commissioner's decision on Beesands Green, Devon (1980) 209/D/1 35-6, following a High Court opinion on the case.

58. It has been suggested by some commentators that the date given in the application for registration must reflect a period of at least 20 years immediately preceding the application. In fact, there is no such requirement. The question posed by part 4 of application Form 30 is: on what date did the land become a town or village green? For 'traditional' greens (ie those with long-standing use by local inhabitants), a period of use which could have supported a claim for registration under the original exercise will not on its own justify a new claim now. An entirely fresh 20-year period of use, ending after 1970, needs to be identified in order to demonstrate the necessary 'event' by which the land 'becomes' a green.

59. So the most appropriate entry in part 4 for traditional greens may be 1 August 1990, assuming there has been clear continuity of use since 31 July 1970. This was the date after which unregistered greens ceased to be recognised by the 1965 Act. A fresh 20-year period of use after July 1970 can be relied upon to requalify the land for registration.[1]

60. As well as specifying the date on which land is deemed actually to have become a green through the passing of 20 years' use, the application should assist the registration authority by making it clear whether qualifying use continues up to the date of application – and if not, when it ceased, and in what circumstances.

61. Once at least 20 years' use has elapsed, new obstructions to lawful sports and pastimes, or attempts to exclude local inhabitants from the land, will not of themselves invalidate a claim. But the longer such obstruction or exclusion has been accepted by the local inhabitants, the more this may call into question the notion that their original use was as of right.

62. For 'newer' greens on which qualifying use began too late to make them registrable under the original process, part 4 of the application could in fact cite any date after January 1970 on which the period of at least 20 years actually expired. For example, if use actually began on 1 March 1952, the date shown on the form could be 1 March 1972. Again, it is important also to show whether use has continued to the present day or, if not, when it ceased and why.

Customary rights of recreation

63. The courts have long recognised customary rights of recreation for local inhabitants in specific cases. Commentators to date have tended to argue that the 1965 Act extinguished such rights wherever the land in question was not successfully registered during the period 1967-70. They argue this because section 1(2) (a) of the 1965 Act says that land unregistered at July 1970 shall not 'be deemed to be' a town or village green.

64. In reality, many genuine greens did not end up registered as such, for a wide range of reasons including the fact that many were instead registered as common land, which prevented their registration as greens. George Laurence QC, in an opinion to the Countryside Commission, has refuted the idea that the non-registration of 'traditional' greens extinguished customary recreational rights over such land:

> *I do not accept the argument that deeming land 'not to be a town or village green' (in the 1965 Act sense of that expression) entails deeming it to be* **neither** *land allotted by or under an act for the exercise and recreation of local inhabitants,* **nor** *land on which the local inhabitants have a customary right to indulge in lawful sports and pastimes,* **nor** *land on which the local inhabitants have indulged in such sports or pastimes as of right for not less than 20 years. Such a reading would have the effect of depriving local inhabitants of their customary or statutory rights, which I do not believe to have been Parliament's intention . . . If Parliament had wanted to say that people's rights were adversely affected by non-registration, it should have said so . . . In my opinion, this is what Oliver J thought also when he said, admittedly rather enigmatically, in* Re Turnworth Down, Dorset *(1978) Ch 251 at pp 260, 261, this:*
>
> *'It is not said, it is true, what is the consequence of non-registration of a town or village green, except to the extent that Section 1(2) (a) provides that, after the end of the specified period:*
>
> *"no land capable of being registered under this Act shall be deemed to be common land or a town or village green unless it is so registered".*
>
> *'On the face of it, it seems that the local inhabitants are merely left to*

---

(1) In fact, continuous use of a 'traditional' green until 3 January 1990 (20 years after the registers closed to applications under the original exercise), or even until 6 August 1985 (20 years after the passing of the Registration Act) may have been enough to qualify it for new registration: see the *New Windsor* case. But assuming that qualifying use in a particular case had actually continued to 1 August 1990, it would make sense for the applicant to cite this date in the application. This would avoid any complex legal questions arising over the relevance of use which took place before the end of the original registration process.

bear with such fortitude as they can command the fact that the land . . . is not deemed to be a town or village green.'

I read Oliver J as saying in that passage that the inhabitants will need very little fortitude indeed because, despite the fact that their town or village green is not on the register, their rights to enjoy it remain undisturbed.

65. Assuming that there is not already a pre-1965 Act judgment confirming that such customary recreational rights exist in a particular case,[1] the local inhabitants have the option of seeking a High Court declaration that they do hold such rights over an area of land. In seeking this, they may ask for an injunction to restrain interference with the exercise of these rights, and if necessary for an order to restore land to its former condition. Rule 12 of Rules of the Supreme Court Order 15 governs the procedure.

66. Such an application may be made by one or more inhabitants of the locality, or their representatives, or by the Attorney-General, or by any of the relevant local authorities including the parish or town council.[2]

67. In making such an application to the High Court, there is nothing to prevent the applicant from relying exclusively on use prior to 1970. An application for the recognition of customary recreational rights is an entirely separate matter from a claim for registration as a green, and does not formally need to demonstrate recent use for 20 years. It can relate to much earlier use, if appropriate – as it did in the *New Windsor* case – so long as firm evidence of this prior use exists.

68. According to legal theory, demonstrating customary rights involves proving use dating back to time immemorial – usually expressed as the year 1189. This is not as formidable a task as it sounds:

Whatever definition you may give to custom and prescription, we all know that they are legal fictions invented by judges for the purpose of giving a legal foundation or origin to long usage . . . It is impossible to prove actual usage in all time by living testimony. The usual course taken is this: persons of middle or old age are called, who state that in their time, usually at least half a century, the usage has always prevailed. That is considered, in the absence of countervailing evidence, to

show that the usage has prevailed from all time.[3]

69. The main advantage to the applicant of seeking a judicial decision that customary recreational rights exist – if one can be obtained – is that the rights of local inhabitants to use the land are then clear, incontrovertible and irrevocable, whether exercised thereafter or not. Unless expressly extinguished at some future date by statute or under adequate statutory powers (eg compulsory purchase), the recreational rights would continue in force. They would also rule out incompatible new uses of the land, including development.

70. Set against these possible advantages is the considerable cost, commitment and risk which is involved in going to court for such a ruling, which may not in the event be obtainable in a particular case. The alternative is for a representative of the inhabitants to apply for registration of the land as a new green under the 1965 Act, using the procedure considered in the rest of this manual. It is suggested later (see 'Effect of new registration') that the new registration process may in practice achieve a similar result.

71. It may seem odd to describe land as 'becoming' a town or village green, and thereby justifying new registration in accordance with section 13(b) of the 1965 Act, if it has in reality been within the definition of a green all along. But although the Act did not extinguish any customary rights which then existed, it did set a clear date – 31 July 1970 – after which unregistered town or village greens were not recognised as such by the Act.

72. After 31 July 1970, therefore, the clock started running again. So long as there is good evidence of qualifying use over a 20-year period ending on or after 1 August 1990, any evidence of more long-standing recreational uses of the land, far from debarring such an application, can only serve to enhance the standing of the claim. But without the new 20-year period of use, the land does not reacquire the ability to be registered, and must remain outside the registers, however strong the prior evidence of town or village green status. Mere discovery of an old court ruling or inclosure award is not enough of an event to justify new registration.

73. The exception to this rule is that a judicial decision made after 2 January 1970, that customary recreational rights exist over a piece of land, may be enough of an event to justify, on its own account, new registration as a town or village

---

(1) An example, where customary recreational rights were found to exist, is the wake or fair at Wraysbury in Berkshire, considered in *Wyld v Silver* (1963) 1 Ch 243, CA.

(2) *Wyld v Silver* (1963) 1 Ch 243, CA. *New Windsor Corporation v Mellor* (1975) 1 Ch 380; (1975) 3 All ER 44, CA. Local Government Act 1972 s222. *Stoke-on-Trent Council v B & Q Ltd* (1984) AC 754, 771-775. *Kent County Council v Batchelor (no 2)* (1979) 1 WLR 213.

(3) *Hammerton v Honey* (1876) 24 WR 603, Jessel MR.

green, according to notes 5 and 8 to Form 30. Registration would be under the second arm of the greens definition reproduced in paragraph 4. No specific proof of 20 years' recent use would be required to justify registration in this case, because the judicial decision itself would supply the necessary 'event' by which the land became a green for the purposes of the 1965 Act. These grounds have not been tested in court, to the Society's knowledge.

74. The current official circular on new registration – Circular 2/70 (3/70 in Wales) gives misleading guidance about the ability of 'traditional' greens to reacquire their ability to be registered. It says:

> *The regulations do not apply to land which became . . . a green before 3 January 1970. (Paragraph 3)*
>
> *A green which has been used as of right for sports and pastimes for 20 years or upwards before 3 January 1970 should have been registered in the initial period under Section 4 of the Act, and application for its registration under these Regulations should be rejected.*

75. The Department of Environment's Directorate of Rural Affairs is understood to have accepted informally that, a quarter of a century after it was written, this guidance has become misleading. So long as an event has genuinely occurred after 2 January 1970 which causes land to 'become' a town or village green for the purpose of the Act – or, as the title note to Form 30 rather more aptly expresses it, to 'become registrable' as a green once more – there is in fact no bar to registration. Even though the official circular carries no weight in interpreting the law, it is desirable that the guidance it offers should now be corrected.

Registration as green following removal from common land register

76. One of the difficulties of the registration system introduced by the 1965 Act was that there were many pieces of land within or near settlements which were, on the face of it, eligible for registration either as a town or village green, or as common land, because:

- *on the one hand, they had a well-established pattern of local recreational use which could have supported registration of the green;*
- *on the other hand, they were registrable as a common because they had rights of common exercisable over them or because, being open, uncultivated, unoccupied land, they*

were classed as 'waste land of a manor' for the purposes of the second arm of the common land definition at section 22(1) of the 1965 Act.

77. However, regulations and guidance on the Act quickly established that, where land was provisionally registered as both common and green, the two registrations were to be regarded as conflicting with each other, with the result that at least one of them must fall. This treatment was implied, rather than required, by the 1965 Act proviso that 'common land . . . does not include a town or village green'.

78. In the rush to register all appropriate land within the short designated period of 1967-70, and given the poor drafting of the 1965 Act and the complexity of the legal concepts which were at stake, many misjudgments were made about the way in which particular areas of land should best be registered. Often people would simply go by whether a piece of land had the word 'common' or 'green' in its name, or whether the word was used in local parlance.

79. The results were sometimes unfortunate. In some cases, the existence of two 'conflicting' provisional registrations served to weaken the case for confirming either, and both were eventually removed by the Commons Commissioner. In others, land was recognised by the commissioner as plainly having been placed in the wrong register, but only on one occasion known to the Society (*re Bottoms, near Dry Bridge, South Tawton, Devon,* (1978) 209/D/109) did the commissioner respond by transferring land to the correct register. Normally he would simply cancel the inappropriate registration, noting in passing that the wrong register appeared to have been selected, but regarding himself as unable to do anything about it.

80. If a common land registration remains in place today, the same land may not be newly registered as a town or village green simply in order to place recreational use as of right 'on the record'. Such joint registration is outlawed by regulation 3(2) of the Regulations and by the section 22(1) definition of common land.

81. There is no suggestion however that the existence of a common land registration has any impact on the recreational rights which the local inhabitants may have over an area of land.[1] There is indeed nothing to prevent an application being made for a judicial decision to recognise that customary recreational rights exist over land which is registered as a common. It is only under *registration*

---

(1) As the Commons Commissioner said in his decision on *Rodmersham Green, Kent* (1976) 219/D/19-22, 'Apart from the [1965] Act, the whole or some part of the waste land of a manor can be, and often is, also a village green on which the inhabitants have a customary recreational right.'

law that there is any difficulty over simultaneously recording both types of land status.

82. If a common land registration has been cancelled by the commissioner at the 'provisional' stage, or removed by the registration authority under section 13(a) subsequent to final registration (having 'ceased' to be common land), there is no longer any such bar to new registration of the same land as a green, if there is evidence of 20 years' qualifying use by local inhabitants. An application may therefore be made.

83. It also seems likely that the act of removing a common land registration would itself count as enough of an event to cause qualifying land to become registrable as a town or village green for the purposes of the Act *without* fresh proof of 20 years' recent use. This might apply, for example, if there is clear documentary evidence that the land has the status of a green – perhaps a pre-1965 Act judgment recognising customary recreational rights, or an inclosure award making the land a statutory recreation allotment. In this situation, the post-1970 'event' justifying new registration as a green is the removal of the common land registration, which formerly made registration as a green impossible.

84. The assertion in note 5 to Form 30 that 'land can become a town or village green after 2 January 1970 in one of the following ways . . . ' should not be taken to rule out grounds for new registration which are not listed there.

Registration of 'substituted land'

85. The Regulations provide for the new registration of any 'substituted land' exchanged for a town or village green which is removed from the registers in accordance with an Act of Parliament, eg following a compulsory purchase. Some of the circumstances in which this can occur are set out in note 5 to statutory application Form 30.

86. The Open Spaces Society can provide further information on request about the exchange procedure and requirements.

Registration of highway land

87. Although the 1965 Act makes it clear that no part of a highway may be regarded as common land, there is nothing to stop all or part of a highway being regarded as a town or village green if the circumstances justify this. Areas of open land alongside minor roads frequently do have a long-standing pattern of local recreational use, as opposed to one of mere passage from A to B. Many have already been successfully registered under the Act.

88. Registration has no effect on the highway status of the land. Equally, the 'public' status of a highway does not nullify a claim that all or part of it is a green, so long as it is clear that the recreational use (as opposed to a mere passage along the highway) which takes place there is primarily or exclusively by local people.[1]

Registration of local authority land

89. It has been argued by some local authorities owning land claimed as a green that the authority could not lawfully allow its land to become a green, or otherwise allow its powers over the land to be substantially reduced or constrained or confined. This has not been tested in court but Vivian Chapman of counsel, acting as inspector in the Peartree Green, Southampton, inquiry, rejected such a submission.

90. Local authority objectors to new registration will tend to allege that use was permissive, rather than

---

(1) See for example the Commons Commissioner decisions in *re Medstead Village Green, Hampshire* (1979) 214/D/113 and in *re The Green, Hargrave, Suffolk* (1979) 234/D/79.

as of right. Such a claim can only be judged on the facts. See the section above on 'As of right'.

91. The designation of land as public open space under the Open Spaces Act 1906 in no way inhibits a claim for registration as a town or village green. Again, the claim can only be judged on the facts of the particular case, and in particular on whether use flowed from express permission, or vice versa.

Motivation of applicant or objector

92. The motives of those who apply for new registration as a town or village green, or who object to such registration, are irrelevant to the outcome. Whether people act from altruism, self-interest, a desire to protect land from development or a desire to be troublesome, the job of the registration authority remains the same: to assess the facts of the case, and decide whether or not a claim appears, on the balance of probabilities, to be valid in law.[1]

Registration procedure

Application

93. Any person may apply to register land as a green, using Form 30 (see Appendix 1). A fuller statement of facts should be attached to Form 30, as described below. A covering statutory declaration is also required, in the form shown at the end of Form 30. It needs to be made as described in note 9 to Form 30.

94. The land which has been used for lawful sports and pastimes should be named at part 3 of Form 30. The exact boundaries of the area of land actually used for this purpose should be clearly shown on an attached map or scale plan, drawn in ink on a scale of at least six inches to the mile.

95. Equally, the locality whose inhabitants use the land for this purpose should be named at part 3, and its boundaries clearly shown on a map or plan too.

96. Part 4 of Form 30 should contain the date after 2 January 1970 on which the land is said to have become a green. Identifying this date accurately is important. If use has continued to the present day, this should also be made clear in part 4. See the section 'Not less than 20 years' above.

97. Part 5 of the form asks how the land became a green. The question cannot be answered in the space provided! A statement should be attached to Form 30, and referred to at part 5 setting out clearly:

- *under which arm of the 1965 act section 22(1) definition of 'town or village green' – normally the third – the land is said to have become*

registrable as a green: see paragraph 4 above for the definition;
- *the nature of the 'event' which caused the land to become registrable – eg 20 years' use since 1 August 1970;*
- *what activities have taken place, and over which parts of the land they have taken place, during this period: suitable statements should be attached from those claiming to have taken part or, if there are many, from representatives of them;*
- *examples to demonstrate that use has taken place without force, secrecy or permission: see section on 'As of right' above;*
- *whether there is any longer tradition of use by local inhabitants: details should be supplied, including any specific recollections by older inhabitants.*

98. Evidence forms, such as that at Appendix 3, can be used to provide the information listed above.

99. Authenticated copies (not originals) should be enclosed of any relevant judicial decisions, inclosure awards or other documents which may help to substantiate the claim. These should be listed at part 8 of Form 30. Note however that note 8(3) to the form does not in any way imply that claims of 20 years' use are only valid if supported by a court ruling that such use has in fact taken place. A formal ruling in relation to 20 years' use would be unusual.

100. What matters is to present as fully and accurately as possible what has actually happened on the land during the period in question. If the actual use does not appear to conform to the requirements of the statutory definition of 'town or village green', as explained in detail above, then attempts to make the facts fit the requirements will be fruitless.

Processing of application by registration authority

101. The authority's role in relation to an application is to consider all the facts of the case and decide whether, on the balance of probabilities, the application appears well founded in law. The Commons Commissioner has no role.

102. Registration authorities might like to consider producing a pack for applicants for greens registration. Such a pack could include:

(1)   *Wyld* v *Silver* (1963) 1 Ch 243, CA at 258.

- *an evidence form (an example is at Appendix 3);*

- *an application form (ie Form 30, including statutory declaration format and notes, as reproduced at Appendix 1);*

- *the statutory criteria to be satisfied;*

- *any minimum criteria set by the authority to render the application valid in its view;*

- *reference to this manual for further guidance.*

103. If the registration authority considers an application 'not to be duly made' (regulation 5(7)), it may reject it. This appears to refer to identifying at the outset any technical or procedural deficiencies in an application, rather than to forming an instant opinion on the relevant matters of law. If there is scope for the applicant to put the technical or procedural deficiencies right, the registration authority must give him reasonable opportunity to do so, rather than simply rejecting the application.

104. It is also open to the registration authority (see regulation 3(7)(d)(ii)) to call at any point for further supporting evidence, if it reasonably requires this in order to decide the application.

105. Once the registration authority is satisfied with the application, it must advertise it so as to secure sufficient publicity, eg by notices in local newspapers, and by posting notices on the land itself. Notice must also be given on Form 33 to anyone with a legal interest in the land, or who is likely to wish to object to the application (regulation 4). At least six weeks must be allowed for any written objections to be submitted (regulation 5).

106. On receiving any such objections, the authority must send them to the applicant. It must give him a reasonable opportunity to deal with the matters raised.

107. If the registration authority believes there are *prima facie* grounds for rejecting the application, it must give the applicant a reasonable opportunity to deal with these before taking any decision on the application: see regulation 6(3).

Consideration of application by registration authority

108. Consideration should focus exclusively on legal issues, rather than amenity or property considerations. This makes a committee, such as that used to decide planning applications, an inappropriate vehicle for determining applications. Indeed, the process for dealing with applications to register new greens closely resembles that for applications to add paths to the definitive map. The decision to be made turns on evidence, not on policy considerations.

109. Therefore it is preferable that the relevant committee should:

- *give a standing delegation to officers to determine applications on their legal merits;*

- *agree an internal procedure based on the one set out in the Regulations and described above;*

- *set criteria as to circumstances in which an inspector should be appointed and a public inquiry held (see below).*

110. In contested or difficult cases, it is good practice for the registration authority to appoint an inspector, usually experienced counsel from the Chancery Bar, to hold a public inquiry. The inspector hears all the parties and considers all the evidence, and then reports and recommends to the registration authority. The authority is not bound by the inspector's recommendations, but may generally be expected to adopt them and decide accordingly. Such an inquiry enables an independent judicial element to be injected with an objective result. The expense involved may well be justified in the saving of officer time and in the quality of the decision, which will be very unlikely to be susceptible to judicial review.

111. No strict or legal rules of evidence apply at such an inquiry. The applicant is expected to prove his case on the balance of probabilities. In processing and deciding the claim, the registration authority must act in accordance with the principles of natural justice and proper administration, and must reach the correct legal judgment as to the validity of the application. The applicant and those with a legal interest in the land should receive a copy of the inspector's decision.

112. Public inquiries were held, for example, in the cases of Peartree Green, Southampton (Hampshire County Council); Emmet's Park, Binfield, Berkshire (Berkshire County Council); and Post Hill Quarries, Leeds (Leeds City Council).

113. The relevant committee should set the criteria as to when it will offer applicants and objectors a choice between a public inquiry and written representations. An inquiry should be held if any party wants one. If the matter is dealt with by written representations, each party is invited to comment in writing on the other's case. The inspector (who should be of the calibre recommended in paragraph 110) should make a

'New' greens

Wittersham
village green
near Rye in
Kent, registered
in 1993

Photo:
Mavis King

Duncan Down
village green,
near Whitstable
in Kent,
registered in
1992. This view
is to the north-
east.

Photo:
Peggy Starkey

The Fields,
Kings Norton,
Birmingham,
registered in
1994

Photo:
Sue Thomas

**Bonnington
village green,
south of Ashford
in Kent, was
registered in
1992**

Photo:
Kent County Council

**Charing in Kent.
Clewards Meadow t
the right of the
church was
registered in 1991**

Photo:
Kent County Council

**Duncan Down,
near Whitstable
in Kent,
winter 1993/4**

Photo:
Peggy Starkey

village green
in Kent. View
north over
Whitstable to
the sea

Photo:
Peggy Starkey

**Satley village green,
south of Consett in
County Durham,
registered in 1993**

Photo:
Durham County Council

**Low Pittington
village green,
north-west of
Durham in
County Durham,
registered in
1994**

Photo:
Durham County Council

Background:
**Tobogganing on
Duncan Down in
Kent in the 1930s**

Photo:
Cliff Court

**Green at Steepfield,
Hebden Bridge,
West Yorks, registered
in 1991**

Photo:
Polly Webber

Wittersham village green near Rye in Kent, registered in 1993

Photo:
Mavis King

'The Fields' at Kings Norton, Birmingham, registered in 1994

Photo:
Sue Thomas

site visit. His decision should be sent to all with a legal interest in the land, and it should be clear who the inspector was.

Rejection

114. If the application is rejected, the authority must inform the applicant of the reasons for the rejection. However, a rejected registration need not necessarily be the end of the matter. It remains open to the applicant (or anyone else) to make a fresh application, for example one offering further legal arguments for registration, or citing a different locality or period of use.

115. While there is no formal right of appeal under the 1965 Act against a rejected application, it is open to the applicant to seek a judicial review of the authority's conduct if he believes it to constitute an abuse of power or to be wrong in law, unreasonable, procedurally improper, biased, or contrary to his own or the inhabitants' legitimate expectations.[1]

Acceptance

116. If an application is accepted, the authority registers the land as a town or village green. There is no 'provisional' stage of registration, as there was under the original exercise. It must send details of the registration to the applicant.

Effect of new registration

117. Registration of a town or village green does not of itself confer any recreational rights which did not already exist prior to registration.[2] Indeed, in the *New Windsor* case Lord Denning asserted that 'at common law, 20-year user gives no rights'. Under the local law of custom (as distinct from the general common law), however, 20-year user as of right *does* establish that customary rights exist.[3]

118. It was on this account that the third arm was added to the greens definition reproduced in paragraph 4 above. The official notes on clauses for this definition stated 'the provision has been made that a customary right of recreation shall be capable of being established on proof of 20 years' user'. Some Commons Commissioner decisions have expressly acknowledged the creation of a customary right in this way.[4]

119. A new registration under the third arm of the greens definition will only be accepted by a registration authority if 20 years' user by local inhabitants, as of right, for lawful sports and pastimes, has been proved. Registration represents conclusive

evidence of the matters registered (section 10, 1965 Act). Notwithstanding what is said in the *New Windsor* case, therefore, the practical effect of the registration authority accepting land onto the register appears to be to confirm the existence of customary recreational rights for the inhabitants of the locality over the land.

120. The exact nature of these local rights is not evident from the register itself, and will vary from case to case, depending on the activities which have actually taken place over the years on the land. These activities will have been reflected (perhaps not exhaustively) in the application to register, but are not specified in the register entry. Neither is the relevant locality stated in the register.

121. Where registration took place under the first or second arm of the greens definition, the actual right and relevant locality may be documented on the relevant inclosure award or court judgment. Again, though, the register itself does not reveal either, or even state under which arm of the definition the land was registered.

---

(1) *Council for Civil Service Unions* v *Minister for Civil Service* (1985) AC 374.
(2) *New Windsor Corporation* v *Mellor* (1975) 1 Ch 380.
(3) In *R* v *Joliffe* (1823) 2 B&C 54, and *Brocklebank* v *Thompson* (1903) 2 Ch 344 at 350, it was held that 'a regular usage of 20 years, unexplained and uncontradicted, is sufficient to warrant a jury finding the existence of an immemorial custom'.
(4) See for example the Commons Commissioner's decision *re Rodmersham Green, Kent* (1976) 219/D/19-22.

122. While this outcome is far from perfect, registration does at least log the existence of some kind of area-wide recreational right over the land. For those seeking to preserve such land as a local amenity and open space, this is very important.

- *It ensures that prospective new owners are aware from the outset of the established recreational function of the land, so helping to avoid any future conflicts of opinion.*

- *It substantially reduces the likelihood of future changes to the management or use of the land which would be incompatible with its recreational use, both by influencing local planners and by acknowledging (by implication) the scope for civil action to deal with obstructions and interference in the manner described in paragraph 65.*[1]

123. Two important nineteenth-century protective provisions may also be deemed to apply to all registered greens, since registration following at least 20 years' user as of right effectively acknowledges the existence of a customary recreational right.

124. Section 12 of the Inclosure Act 1857 makes it an offence to do anything which injures a green or interrupts its use or enjoyment as a place for exercise and recreation. Section 29 of the Commons Act 1876 makes all types of encroachment, inclosure and building an offence unless they are for the better enjoyment of the green. Both sections are reproduced at Appendix 5.

125. Once established, customary (or statutory) recreational rights for the inhabitants of a locality cannot be abandoned or lost by disuse.[2] They may only be removed by statute, or under statutory powers (eg of compulsory purchase) which are adequate for the purpose. They will not be affected by extraneous factors such as subsequent use by members of the public. They persist even if the land has been developed, eg as a car park or building.[3] It follows that a registered green cannot cease to be such for the purposes of section 13(a) of the 1965 Act, other than through some kind of statutory process.

Further advice

126. The Open Spaces Society can offer advice to its individual and corporate members on the issues raised in this manual, and on associated matters, such as ownership and management of greens.

127. The Society also knows of a number of solicitors, barristers and academic lawyers with knowledge and experience of town and village green law and practice, some of whom have directly or indirectly assisted the Society.

---

(1) See for example *Corporation of Truro* v *Rowe* (1901) 2 KB 870 on the limitations imposed on other uses of the land.
(2) *Wyld* v *Silver* (1963) 1 Ch 243 CA.
(3) *Wyld* v *Silver* (1963) 1 Ch 243 CA. *New Windsor Corporation* v *Mellor* (1975) 1 Ch 380.

Appendices
1 - 7

Appendix 1
The Commons Registration (New Land) Regulations 1969
SI 1843, Form 30, statutory declaration
form and notes

S T A T U T O R Y   I N S T R U M E N T S

1969 No. 1843

COMMON

The Commons Registration (New Land) Regulations 1969

Made	- - - 19th December 1969
Laid before Parliament	2nd January 1970
Coming into Operation	3rd January 1970

The Minister of Housing and Local Government and the Secretary of State, in exercise of their respective powers under paragraphs (*a*) and (*b*) of section 13, paragraphs (*a*), (*b*), (*g*), (*i*) and (*k*) of subsection (1), and subsections (2) and (4) of section 19 of the Commons Registration Act 1965(**a**), as read with the Ministry of Land and Natural Resources (Dissolution) Order 1967(**b**), and of all other powers enabling them in that behalf, hereby make the following Regulations:—

Title and commencement

1. These Regulations may be cited as the Commons Registration (New Land) Regulations 1969, and shall come into operation on 3rd January 1970.

Interpretation

2.—(1) The Interpretation Act 1889(**c**) applies for the interpretation of these Regulations as it applies for the interpretation of an Act of Parliament.

(2) In these Regulations, unless the context otherwise requires,—

"the Act" means the Commons Registration Act 1965;

"application" means an application under these Regulations;

"concerned authority", in relation to an application to a registration authority, means a local authority (other than the registration authority) in whose area any part of the land affected by the application lies;

"Form 6" means the form so numbered in the General Regulations or a form to substantially the same effect, and "Form" followed by a number above 28 means the form so numbered in the Schedule to these Regulations, or a form to substantially the same effect;

"the General Regulations" means the Commons Registration (General) Regulations 1966(**d**) as amended (**e**), and "General Regulation" followed by a number means the regulation so numbered in the General Regulations;

"Model Entry" followed by a number means the specimen entry so numbered in Part 1 of Schedule 2 to the General Regulations, and "Standard Entry" followed by a number means the specimen entry so numbered in Part 2 of that Schedule, or an entry to substantially the same effect;

(**a**) 1965 c. 64.   (**b**) S.I. 1967/156 (1967 I, p. 258).
(**c**) 1889 c. 63.
(**d**) S.I. 1966/1471 (1966 III, p. 3978).
(**e**) The amending instruments are S.I 1968/658, 1968/989 (1968 I, p. 1490; 1968 II, p. 2615).

[H.L.G. 45068]

"provisional registration" means a registration under section 4 of the Act which has not become final;

"substituted land" and, in relation to any substituted land, "the taken land", bear the same meanings as in General Regulation 28.

(3) A requirement upon a registration authority to publish a document in any area is a requirement to cause the document to be published in such one or more newspapers circulating in that area as shall appear to the authority sufficient to secure adequate publicity for it.

(4) A requirement to display a document or copies thereof is a requirement to treat it, for the purposes of section 287 of the Local Government Act 1933(**a**) (public notices), as if it were a public notice within that section.

(5) Where the day or the last day on which anything is required or permitted by or in pursuance of these Regulations to be done is a Sunday, Christmas Day, Good Friday, bank holiday or a day appointed for public thanksgiving or mourning, the requirement or permission shall be deemed to relate to the first day thereafter which is not one of the days before-mentioned.

(6) Any requirement (however expressed) that a registration authority shall send anything to "the applicant" shall, where a solicitor has been instructed for the purposes of an application, be deemed to be satisfied by sending it to the solicitor, or, where two or more persons are concerned together in an application and no solicitor has been instructed, to that one of them whose name appears first in the application form.

(7) A requirement upon a registration authority to stamp any document is a requirement to cause an impression of its official stamp as described in General Regulation 3 to be affixed to it, and that the impression shall bear the date mentioned in the requirement or (where no date is mentioned) the date when it was affixed.

(8) An indication in any form in the Schedule to these Regulations that the form shall bear the official stamp of a registration authority is a requirement upon the authority to stamp it.

Land becoming common land or a town or village green

3.—(1) Where, after 2nd January 1970, any land becomes common land or a town or village green, application may be made subject to and in accordance with the provisions of these Regulations for the inclusion of that land in the appropriate register and for the registration of rights of common thereover and of persons claiming to be owners thereof.

(2) Where any land is for the time being registered under the Act, no application shall be entertained for its registration under these Regulations, and, where any land is for the time being registered under section 4 of the Act (whether or not the registration has become final) no application shall be entertained for the registration of rights of common over it.

(3) No person shall be registered under these Regulations as the owner of any land which is registered under the Land Registration Acts 1925 to 1966(**b**) and no person shall be registered under these Regulations as the owner of any other land unless the land itself is registered under these Regulations.

(4) An application for the registration of any land as common land or as a town or village green may be made by any person, and a registration authority

(**a**) 1933 c. 51.   (**b**) 1925 c. 21; 1936 c. 26; 1966 c. 39.

2

shall so register any land in any case where it registers rights over it under these Regulations.

(5) An application for the registration of a right of common over land which is registered, or which is capable of being registered, under these Regulations, may be made by the owner of the right, or by any person entitled by law to act, in relation to the right, on the owner's behalf or in his stead, or, where the right belongs to an ecclesiastical benefice of the Church of England which is vacant, by the Church Commissioners.

(6) An application for the registration of a claim to the ownership of any land registered under these Regulations may be made by the owner of the land, or by any person entitled by law to act, in relation to the land, on the owner's behalf or in his stead, or, where the land belongs to an ecclesiastical benefice of the Church of England which is vacant, by the Church Commissioners.

(7) An application must be—

(a) in Form 29, 30, 31 or 32 as appropriate;

(b) signed by or on behalf of every applicant who is an individual, and by the secretary or some other duly authorised officer of every applicant which is a body corporate or unincorporate;

(c) accompanied by such documents (if any) as may be requisite under regulation 4 below;

(d) supported—

(i) by a statutory declaration as set out in the appropriate form of application, with such adaptations as the case may require, to be made by the applicant, or by one of the applicants if there is more than one, or by his or their solicitor, or, if the applicant is a body corporate or unincorporate, or charity trustees, by its or their solicitor or by the person who signed the application; and

(ii) by such further evidence, if any, as, at any time before finally disposing of the application, the registration authority may reasonably require.

Documents to accompany applications

4.—(1) Subject to paragraph (2) below, every application must be accompanied by, or by a copy or sufficient abstract of, every document relating to the matter which the applicant has in his possession or under his control, or of which he has a right to the production.

(2) In the case of an application for the registration of any rights of common, or of a claim to the ownership of any land, the applicant shall not be obliged to furnish to the registration authority, or to disclose the existence of, any document which he would not be obliged to abstract or produce to a purchaser under a contract for the sale by the applicant of the rights or the land made otherwise than by correspondence and containing no stipulations as to title.

Disposal of applications

5.—(1) On receiving an application, the registration authority shall allot a distinguishing number to it, and shall mark the application form with that number.

(2) Where a registration authority receives an application for the registration of a right of common affecting any coal or anthracite it shall, before entertain-

ing the application, serve notice in writing to that effect upon the National Coal Board, giving the name and address of the applicant and particulars of the right of common, of the land over which it is exercisable and of the land (if any) to which it is attached.

(3) The registration authority shall send the applicant a receipt for his application containing a statement of the number allotted thereto; and Form 6, if used for that purpose, shall be sufficient.

(4) Subject to paragraph (7) below, a registration authority shall, on receipt of an application,—

(a) send a notice in Form 33, 34 or 35, as appropriate, to every person (other than the applicant) whom the registration authority has reason to believe (whether from information supplied by the applicant or otherwise) to be an owner, lessee, tenant or occupier of any part of the land affected by the application, or to be likely to wish to object to the application;

(b) publish in the concerned area, and display, such a notice as aforesaid, and send the notice and a copy of the application to every concerned authority;

(c) affix such a notice to some conspicuous object on any part of the land which is open, unenclosed and unoccupied, unless it appears to the registration authority that such a course would not be reasonably practicable.

(5) The date to be inserted in any notice under paragraph (4) above by which statements in objection to an application must be submitted to the registration authority shall be such as to allow an interval of not less than six weeks from the latest of the following dates, that is to say, the date on which the notice is displayed by the registration authority, or is published, or may reasonably be expected to be delivered in due course of post or to be displayed under paragraph (6) below.

(6) Every concerned authority receiving, under this regulation, a notice and a copy of an application shall forthwith display copies of the notice, and shall keep the copy of the application available for public inspection at all reasonable times until informed by the registration authority of the disposal of the application.

(7) Where an application appears to a registration authority after preliminary consideration not to be duly made, the authority may reject it without complying with paragraph (4) above, but where it appears to the authority that any action by the applicant might put the application in order, the authority shall not reject the application under this paragraph without first giving the applicant a reasonable opportunity of taking that action.

(8) In this regulation "concerned area" means, in the case of a registration authority which is the council of a county borough, an area including the area of the county borough and the area of every concerned authority, and in any other case, an area including the area of every concerned authority.

Consideration of objections

6.—(1) As soon as possible after the date by which statements in objection to an application have been required to be submitted, the registration authority shall proceed to the further consideration of the application, and the consideration of statements (if any) in objection thereto, in accordance with the following provisions of this regulation.

(2) The registration authority shall not consider any statement in objection to an application unless it is in writing and signed by or on behalf of the person making it, but, subject as aforesaid, the authority shall consider every statement in objection to an application which it receives before the date on which it proceeds to the further consideration of the application under paragraph (1) above, and may consider any such statement which it receives on or after that date and before the authority finally disposes of the application.

(3) The registration authority shall send the applicant a copy of every statement which it is required under paragraph (2) above to consider, and of every statement which it is permitted under that paragraph to consider and intends to consider, and shall not reject the application without giving the applicant a reasonable opportunity of dealing with the matters contained in the statements of which copies are sent to him under this paragraph and with any other matter in relation to the application which appears to the authority to afford prima facie grounds for rejecting the application.

Method of registration

7.—(1) Where a registration authority accepts an application, it shall make the necessary registration, following as closely as possible whichever of the Model Entries 4 and 7 to 12 may be applicable, with such variations and adaptations as the circumstances may require, but with the substitution, for the words "(Registration provisional)", of the words "(Registration under section 13 of the Act)".

(2) The provisions of paragraphs (2) to (7) of General Regulation 10 shall apply to registrations under these Regulations as they apply to provisional registrations.

(3) The provisions of regulation 9 of the Commons Registration (Objections and Maps) Regulations 1968(a) (changes as to provisional register maps) shall apply for the purposes of section 13 of the Act as they apply for the purposes of section 4 thereof, and, accordingly, the following shall be substituted for the definition of "registration" in regulation 2(2) of the said regulations :—

"'registration', except in regulation 9 below, means registration under section 4 of the Act, and 'registered' shall be construed accordingly ;".

(4) Where a registration authority has made a registration under this regulation, it shall file the application form and any plan thereto which is not required for the purpose of General Regulation 20 (supplemental maps) and shall return all other documents which accompanied the application form to the applicant.

Information about disposal of applications, and procedure on rejection

8.—(1) When a registration authority has disposed of an application and, if it has accepted the application, has made the necessary registration, it shall give written notice of the fact to every concerned authority, to the applicant and to every person whose address is known to the registration authority and who objected to the application, and such notice shall include, where the registration authority has accepted the application, details of the registration, and, where it has rejected the application, the reasons for the rejection.

(2) A person shall be taken to have objected to an application for the purposes of paragraph (1) above if he submitted a statement in objection to the

(a) S.I. 1968/989 (1968 II, p. 2615).

---

application which the registration authority was required to consider under paragraph (2) of regulation 6 above or which it did consider under that paragraph.

(3) Where a registration authority has rejected an application, it shall return the application form and all accompanying documents to the applicant.

Substituted land

9.—(1) Where under these Regulations a registration authority registers any substituted land in a register, and the taken land is registered in that register, then—

(a) if no application has been duly made under General Regulation 27 for the removal of the taken land from the register, the authority shall nevertheless amend the register in relation to the taken land as shown in Standard Entry 6 ;

(b) if such an application has been duly made, the registration authority shall not be required to comply with paragraphs (5) to (8) of General Regulation 27 (except so much of paragraph (7) thereof as requires the register to be amended in accordance with Standard Entry 6).

(2) In General Regulation 28(1) (which prohibits the removal of any taken land from a register until the substituted land has been registered under the Act, unless the substituted land is exempt from registration under section 11 of the Act) the words "unless it is exempt from registration under section 11 thereof" are hereby revoked, but without prejudice to their effect in relation to applications and registrations under section 4 of the Act.

Land descriptions

10.—(1) Land must be described for the purposes of any application—

(a) by a plan accompanying the application and referred to therein ; or

(b) in the case of land already registered under the Act, by a reference to the register sufficient to enable the land to be identified ; or

(c) in the case of land to which rights of common are attached, by reference to the numbered parcels on the most recent edition of the ordnance map (quoting the edition).

(2) Any plan accompanying an application must—

(a) be drawn to scale ;

(b) be in ink or other permanent medium ;

(c) be on a scale of not less, or not substantially less, than six inches to one mile ;

(d) show the land to be described by means of distinctive colouring ; and

(e) be marked as an exhibit to the statutory declaration in support of the application.

Official stamp of registration authority indicating date of receipt

Application No.

Register unit No(s):

VG

VG

This section for official use only

COMMONS REGISTRATION ACT 1965, SECTION 13

APPLICATION FOR THE REGISTRATION OF LAND WHICH BECAME A TOWN OR VILLAGE GREEN AFTER 2nd JANUARY 1970

IMPORTANT NOTE:—Before filling in this form, read carefully the notes at the end. An incorrectly completed application form may have to be rejected.

[1]Insert name of registration authority

To the[1]

Application is hereby made for the registration as a town or village green of the land described below, which became so registrable after 2nd January 1970.

Part 1.

(Give Christian names or forenames and surname or, in the case of a body corporate or unincorporate, the full title of the body. If part 2 is not completed all correspondence and notices will be sent to the first named applicant.)

Name and address of the applicant or (if more than one) of every applicant.

Part 2.

(This part should be completed only if a solicitor has been instructed for the purposes of the application. If it is completed, all correspondence and notices will be sent to the solicitor.)

Name and address of solicitor, if any.

Part 3.

Particulars of the land to be registered, i.e. the land claimed to have become a town or village green.

Name by which usually known

Locality

Colour on plan herewith

Part 4.

On what date did the land become a town or village green?

Part 5.

How did the land become a town or village green?

Part 6.

Name and address of every person whom the applicant believes to be an owner, lessee, tenant or occupier of any part of the land claimed to have become a town or village green. (If none are known, write "none".)

Part 7.

For applications to register substituted land (see Note 5); to be disregarded in other cases.

Particulars of the "taken land", i.e. the land which ceased to be a town or village green (or part thereof) when the land described in part 3 became a town or village green (or part).

Name by which usually known

Locality

Colour on plan herewith (if any)

If registered under the 1965 Act, register unit No(s).

Part 8.

List of supporting documents sent herewith, if any. (If none are sent, write "none".)

STATUTORY DECLARATION IN SUPPORT

To be made by the applicant, or by one of the applicants, or by his or their solicitor, or, if the applicant is a body corporate or unincorporate, by its solicitor or by the person who signed the application.

¹*Insert full name (and address if not given in the application form).*

²*Delete and adapt as necessary.*

³*Insert name if applicable.*

I¹, ...
solemnly and sincerely declare as follows:—

1.² I am ((the person) (one of the persons) who (has) (have) signed the foregoing application)) ((the solicitor to (the applicant) (³ .... one of the applicants)).

2. I have read the Notes to the application form.

3. The facts set out in the application form are to the best of my knowledge and belief fully and truly stated and I am not aware of any other fact which should be brought to the attention of the registration authority as likely to affect its decision on this application, nor of any document relating to the matter other than those (if any) mentioned in parts **8** and **9** of the application.

⁴*Insert "marking" as on plan.*

4. The plan now produced and shown to me marked⁴" ...." is the plan referred to in part 3 of the application.

⁵*Delete this paragraph if there is no plan referred to in part 7.*

5.⁵ The plan now produced and shown to me marked⁴" ...." is the plan referred to in part 7 of the application.

And I make this solemn declaration, conscientiously believing the same to be true, and by virtue of the Statutory Declarations Act 1835.

Declared by the said ....

.... ⎫
at .... ⎬ *Signature of Declarant*
in the .... ⎭

this .... day of .... 19......

Before me,

Signature ....

Address ....

Qualification ....

REMINDER TO OFFICER TAKING DECLARATION:
Please initial all alterations and mark any plan as an exhibit.

Part 9.

If there are any other facts relating to the application which ought to be brought to the attention of the registration authority (in particular if any person interested in the land is believed to dispute the claim that it has become a town or village green) full particulars should be given here.

Date .... 19 .

²*The application must be signed by or on behalf of each individual applicant, and by the secretary or some other duly authorised officer of any applicant which is a body corporate or unincorporate.*

Signatures² ....

....

....

....

NOTES

1. Registration authorities

The applicant should take care to submit this application to the correct registration authority. This depends on the situation of the land which is claimed to have become a town or village green. The registration authority for land in an administrative county is the county council; for land in a county borough, it is the county borough council, and for land in Greater London, it is the Greater London Council. However if the land in question is partly in the area of one registration authority and partly in that of another, the authorities may by agreement have provided for one of them to be the registration authority for the whole of the land. An applicant concerned with land lying close to the boundary of an administrative area, or partly in one area and partly in another, should therefore enquire whether such an agreement has been made and, if so, which authority is responsible for the land.

2. Who may apply for registration

An application for the registration of any land which has become a town or village green after 2nd January 1970 may be made by any person.

3. No double registration

If the land is already registered under the Act, whether in the Register of Town or Village Greens or in the separate Register of Common Land, and whether the registration is provisional, final, or under section 13 of the Act (which relates to land becoming common land or a town or village green after 2nd January 1970), an application for registration cannot be entertained, but this does not prevent the submission of an application later on, should the existing registration cease for any reason to be effective (as, for example, by the land being removed from the register under section 13 or by a provisional registration being cancelled or failing to achieve finality). If an earlier registration is believed to exist a search of the register may be obtained by means of C.R. Form 21 (a separate form must be used for each register).

4. Meaning of "town or village green"

"Town or village green" is defined in the Commons Registration Act 1965 as land—

(a) which has been allotted by or under any Act for the exercise or recreation of the inhabitants of any locality, or

(b) on which the inhabitants of any locality have a customary right to indulge in lawful sports and pastimes, or

(c) on which the inhabitants of any locality have indulged in such sports and pastimes as of right for not less than twenty years.

While a town or village green can be subject to rights of common, it does not include land which is registered as common land in the separate Register of Common Land maintained under the Act. (There is a separate form available for applying for the registration under the Act of land which became common land after 2nd January 1970.) "Land" includes land covered with water so that a town or village green can, for instance, include a pond.

5. How land can become a town or village green

Land can become a town or village green after 2nd January 1970 in one of the following ways:—

(1) By or under an Act of Parliament otherwise than as substituted land (as to substituted land, see category (4) below).

(2) By customary right established by judicial decision.

(3) By the actual use of the land by the local inhabitants for lawful sports and pastimes as of right for not less than 20 years.

(4) By substitution or exchange for other land which has ceased to be a town or village green under—

(a) sections 147 and 148 of the Inclosure Act 1845; or

(b) paragraph 11 of Schedule 1 to the Acquisition of Land (Authorisation Procedure) Act 1946; or

(c) any other enactment providing, on the exchange of land, for the transfer of rights, trusts or incidents attaching to the land given in exchange from that land to the land taken in exchange and vice versa.

Land in category (4) is referred to in this form as "substituted land", and the land for which it is substituted, and which has ceased to be a town or village green, is referred to as "the taken land". If this application is accepted for registration, and the taken land is registered in the Register of Town or Village Greens maintained by the same registration authority, the taken land will be removed from the register automatically provided the registration authority is satisfied as to the exact areas of both the substituted and the taken land. No separate application in regard to the latter is necessary in such a case.

6. Land descriptions

In addition to the particulars asked for at part 3 of the form, a plan of the land claimed to have become a town or village green must accompany the application. The particulars in part 3 are necessary to enable the registration authority to identify the land concerned, but the main description of the land will be by means of the plan. This must be drawn to scale, in ink or other permanent medium, and be on a scale of not less, and not substantially less, than six inches to one mile. It must show the land by means of distinctive colouring (a coloured edging inside the boundary will usually suffice) and it must be marked as an exhibit to the statutory declaration (see Note 9 below). If the land to be registered is substituted land (see Note 5 above), then a description of the taken land must be given in part 7, and a plan of this area, too, may have to be provided. If the taken land has already been registered under the Act (as it will in most cases) and comprises the whole of the land in one or more register units, a plan is unnecessary provided the register unit number(s) are quoted. If the taken land comprises only part of the land in a register unit a plan may be dispensed with if the land can be described by reference to some physical feature such as a road, river or railway; the description might, for example, read "The land in register unit No...........lying to the south of the road from A to B". Where this method is not practicable, or the taken land is not registered under the Act, it must be described by a plan which must conform to the requirements mentioned above. Where two plans accompany the application, a different colour should be used in each.

7. Grounds of application: evidence

In part 5 should be set out, as concisely as possible, a statement of the facts relied on to show that the land became a town or village green on the date stated in part 4; this date must be after 2nd January 1970, otherwise the application cannot be entertained. The statement should include particulars of every Act of Parliament, statutory order, order of court, deed or other instrument, and of every act or event, which is material for the purpose. The registration authority has power to call for such further evidence in support of the application as it may reasonably require. If the land is substituted land (see Note 5 above) there should be included in part 5 particulars of the enactment and of the compulsory purchase order, order of exchange or other instrument authorising the exchange or substitution, and of the instrument (if any) under which the exchange or substitution actually took place.

8. Supporting documents

The application must be accompanied by the original or (preferably) by a copy or sufficient abstract of every document relating to the matter which the applicant has in his possession or under his control, or of which he has a right to the production. The following are examples of documents which, under this rule, may normally be expected to be among the documents accompanying applications in the particular cases mentioned:—

(1) Where the land is stated to have become a town or village green by virtue of a private or local Act or of a statutory instrument, the award or other instrument of allotment (if any) made thereunder.

(2) Where the land is stated to have become a town or village green by customary right, an office copy of an order of a court of competent jurisdiction embodying a declaration to that effect.

(3) Where the land is stated to have become a town or village green by the actual use of the land by the local inhabitants for lawful sports and pastimes as of right for not less than 20 years, and there is a declaration by a court of competent jurisdiction to that effect, an office copy of the order embodying that declaration.

(4) Where the land is stated to be substituted land (see Note 5 above), the original or a duly authenticated copy (a) of the compulsory purchase order, order of exchange or other instrument authorising the exchange or substitution, and (b) of the instrument (if any) under which the exchange or substitution actually took place.

The foregoing list is not exhaustive and in special cases the applicant may need to consult the registration authority. Applicants are strongly recommended NOT to forward the original of any deed or other private document. Instead, a copy should be supplied, preferably indorsed

(Name of registration authority)

COMMONS REGISTRATION ACT 1965

Notice of application for registration of land claimed to have become (common land) (a town or village green)[1] after 2nd January 1970

To every reputed owner, lessee, tenant or occupier of any part of the land described below, and to all others whom it may concern.

Application has been made to the registration authority, the *(name and address of registration authority)* by *(name and address of applicant)* under section 13 of the Commons Registration Act 1965 for the inclusion in the Register of (Common Land) (Town or Village Greens)[1] of the land described (at Annex A)[2] below, which it is claimed became (common land) (a town or village green)[1] on *(date given in part 4 of Form 29 or 30)* (in substitution for the land described at Annex B below, which, it is claimed, ceased to be (common land) (a town or village green)[1] on that date)[2], under and by virtue of *(account of circumstances, etc., summarised from part 5 of Form 29 or 30)*.

The application, which includes a plan of(   ),[3] may be inspected at *(address where application available)* (and copies of the application and plan(s) may be inspected at the following local authority offices *(insert names and addresses of concerned local authorities, if any)*)[1].

If the registration authority is satisfied that the land described (at Annex A)[2] below has become (common land) (a town or village green)[1] as claimed, it will so register the land, and such registration will be conclusive evidence of the status of the land as at the date of registration. (The land described at Annex B below will then be removed from the register).[2]

Any person wishing to object to the registration of the land as (common land) (a town or village green)[1] (or to the removal from the register of the land described at Annex B below)[2] should send a written and signed statement of the facts on which he bases his objection to *(name and address of registration authority)* so as to arrive not later than[4]

Dated   19   .

(Signature on behalf of registration authority).

(ANNEX A)[2]

Description of the land claimed to have become (common land) (a town or village green)[1]

(ANNEX B)[2]

(Description of the land claimed to have ceased to be (common land) (a town or village green)[1] *including a reference to the register unit number if the land is registered)*[2]

_____
[1]Delete as necessary.   [2]For substituted land cases only.
[3]Insert "the land proposed for registration" or, in a substituted land case where a plan of the taken land is also provided, "both areas".
[4]Insert date in accordance with regulation 5(5).

---

with a certificate signed by a solicitor that it has been examined against the original. The applicant should indicate, either on the copy itself or in part 8 of the application, as convenient, who has the original and where it may be inspected. If any document relating to the matter is believed to exist but, neither the original nor a copy can be produced, the fact should be mentioned in part 9 of the application, where particulars of the missing document should be given and its non-production accounted for.

The registration authority has power to call for such further evidence as it may reasonably require.

9. Statutory Declaration

The statutory declaration must be made before a justice of the peace, commissioner for oaths or notary public. The plan (or each plan) accompanying the application and referred to in the statutory declaration must be marked as an exhibit and signed by the officer taking the declaration (initialling is insufficient). A plan is marked by writing on the face in ink an identifying symbol such as the letter 'A'. If there is more than one plan a different identifying letter must be used for each. On the back of the plan should appear these words:

This is the exhibit marked 'A' referred to in the statutory declaration of *(name of declarant)* made this *(date)*   19   before me,

....

(Signature and qualification)

10. Action by registration authority

The registration authority will on receipt of the application send an acknowledgment. If this is not received within 10 days the applicant should communicate with the authority. Unless the application has to be rejected after preliminary consideration, the registration authority will give publicity to it and will consider it further in the light of any objections which may be received. The applicant will be supplied with copies of all objections which fall to be considered and will have an opportunity of answering them. Later, the applicant will be informed whether the application has been accepted or rejected. If it is accepted, the land will be registered as a town or village green, and the applicant will be supplied with particulars of the registration. If it is rejected, the applicant will be notified of the reasons for the rejection.

11. False statements

The making of a false statement for the purposes of this application may render the maker liable to prosecution.

Appendix 2

Lawful sports and pastimes

The concept of lawful sports and pastimes in English law is very wide, based on centuries of experience. They are certain, reasonable and continuous recreational activities. *New Windsor Corporation* v *Mellor* (1975) 1 Ch 380, 386-387, Lord Denning MR. *Lockwood* v *Wood* (1844) 6 QB 50. *Hammerton* v *Honey* (1876) 24 WR 603, Sir George Jessel MR. *Fitch* v *Rawling* (1795) 2 Hy Bl 393; (1775-1802) All ER Rep 571. *Mercer* v *Denne* (1904) 2 Ch 534, 551-553. The judicial and commissioner decisions are numerous. Each case turns on its own particular facts. The following have been found to be within the definition:

archery and shooting. *New Windsor Corporation* v *Mellor* (1975) 1 Ch 380

cricket, formal and informal. *Fitch* v *Rawling* (1795) 2 Hy Bl 393; *Lancashire* v *Hunt* (1894) 10 TLR 310

riding horses and ponies and racing. *Lancashire* v *Hunt* (1894) 10 TLR 310

children playing. *Havercroft Green, Wakefield District, West Yorkshire*, (1976) 270/D/1-4. *The Field, Smailes Lane, Rowland Gill, Gateshead Borough, Tyne and Wear* (1984) 266/D/1. *Bridge Green, Hargrave, West Suffolk* (1972) 35/D/1.

village dancing. *Abbot* v *Weekly* (1665) 1 Lev 176

maypole celebrations. *Hall* v *Nottingham* (1875) 1 Ex D 1

fishing. *Top Jetty, Woody Bay, Martinhoe, Devon* (1972) 9/D/9

football, rounders and cricket. *Virgo* v *Harford* (1893) *The Times* 30 March 1893

idling by the river by way of walking, fishing and picnicking. *Foreshore on the east bank of the River Ouse, Naburn, Selby District, North Yorkshire* (1988) 268/D/449

sketching and drawing and painting and bird watching. *Top Jetty, Woody Bay, Martinhoe, Devon* (1972) 9/D/9

local adults picnicking, taking dogs for walks, and fishing in the pond. *White Lane Pond, Four Doles and Clay Pits, Thorne and Stainforth, South Yorkshire (no 1)* (1984) 269/D/36-39

walking the dog, though for the benefit of humans, not the dog. *River Don and its banks, Kirk Bramwith, South Yorkshire* (1984) 269/D/82-92. *White Lane Pond, Four Doles and Clay Pits, Thorne and Stainforth, South Yorkshire (no 1)* (1984) 269/D/36-39

wandering or promenading by way of pastime, recreational walking. 'Popular amusement takes many shapes; and there is no outdoor recreation so general and perennial as the promenade.' *Abercromby* v *Fermoy Town Commissioners* (1900) 1 IR 302, 314, Holmes LJ, following *Dyce* v *Lady James Hay* (1852) 1 Macq 305, HL, Lord St Leonards LC, approved in *Attorney-General* v *Antrobus* (1905) 2 Ch 188, 207, Farwell J. But walking across land, to get from A to B, rather than just wandering about, would seem to indicate a right, or claim to a right, of way – an easement, not a lawful sport or pastime.

The lawful sports and pastimes cited need not have existed since 1189 or time immemorial, because in the nature of things over the years habits and customs change, including lawful sports and pastimes. *Bridge Green, Hargrave, West Suffolk* (1972) 35/D/1.

The lawful sports and pastimes may be either formal and structured, eg organised team games, or informal and unstructured, eg children playing, a family walking along, even one person walking on his own, flying a kite, walking the dog, picking blackberries.

Taken together, and depending upon their inherent nature, the lawful sports and pastimes must have been exercised continuously, albeit perhaps seasonally, during the period specified in the application. For example: snowballing in the winter, cricket in the summer, blackberrying in the autumn, walking the dog all the year round; the first ten years football, the second ten years rounders or baseball (or softball); and so on.

Car parking does not qualify. *Attorney-General* v *Southampton Corporation* (1970) 21 P and CR 281; (1969) 68 LGR 288. *Attorney-General* v *Poole Corporation* (1938) Ch 23, CA.

Appendix 3

Evidence questionnaire in support of claim for registration as a new green

Name ....

Present address ....

....Postcode .... Telephone ....

Your present occupation ....

Address when you used and/or knew the land[1] to be used by the local inhabitants (if applicable) ....

....

Did you sign the reverse side of 'Map A'[2] confirming it relates to this evidence provided by you? ....

By what name was/is the land, shown on 'Map A', known? ....

How many years have you known the land? From .... to ....

Between which years did you use it? From .... to ....

Then from .... to ....

Do you consider yourself to be a local inhabitant with respect to the land? ....

To your knowledge, are there any public paths crossing the land? ....

How often did you use the land (apart from the public paths)? ....

....

What activities did you take part in, and/or how did you use the land? ....

....

Do you know who is the owner/occupier? ....

Are you his/her employee or tenant? ....

Has the owner/occupier seen you on the land? .... What did he/she say? ....

....

Was owner/occupier permission ever sought by you for activities on the land? ....

Have you, or do you know of any local inhabitant who has, been prevented from using the land? .... If yes, when and reason? ....

Has any general attempt ever been made by notice or fencing or by any other means to prevent or discourage the use being made of the land by the local inhabitants? ....

Did you use the land as if you had the right to do so? ....

Are you submitting any photographs or any other evidence of use of the land by local inhabitants? ....

If so, have you signed the reverse side of each item? ....

If not, would you be prepared to lend or show such evidence to the registration authority? ....

Have you made a separate written statement? ....

Have you seen other 'local inhabitants', perhaps friends or relatives, using the land in this way? ....

If you have knowledge of others who may be in a position to complete an evidence form, would you please write their names upon the reverse side.

Signed ....   Date ....

---

(1)   'the land' in this form means 'the claimed land.'

(2)   Map A is the map showing the claimed land, which should accompany the form and which will subsequently accompany the application: see Form 30 part 3 and note 6.

Appendix 4

Likely sequence of events in registering new greens

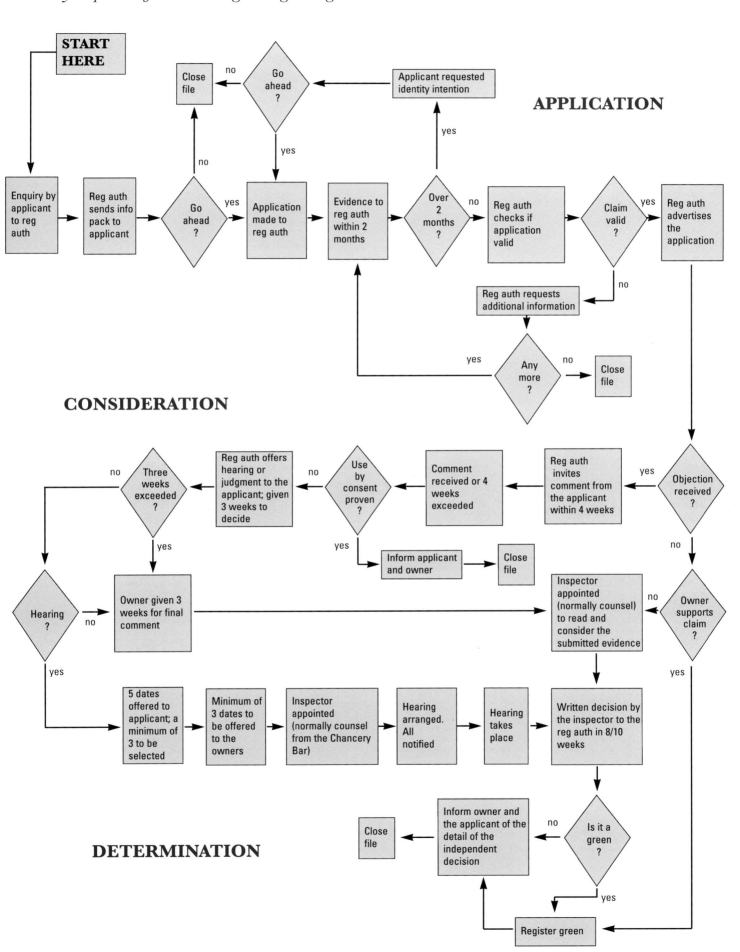

Appendix 5

Inclosure Act 1857 Section 12 and Commons Act 1876 Section 29

Inclosure Act 1857

12. And whereas it is expedient to provide summary means of preventing nuisances in town greens and village greens, and on land allotted and awarded upon any inclosure under the said Acts as a place for exercise and recreation: If any person wilfully cause any injury or damage to any fence of any such town or village green or land, or wilfully and without lawful authority lead or drive any cattle or animal thereon, or wilfully lay any manure, soil, ashes, or rubbish or other matter or thing thereon, or do any other act whatsoever to the injury of such town or village green or land, or to the interruption of the use or enjoyment thereof as a place for exercise and recreation, such person shall for every such offence, upon a summary conviction thereof before two justices, upon the information of any churchwarden or overseer of the parish in which such town or village green or land is situate, or of the person in whom the soil of such town or village green or land may be vested, forfeit and pay, in any of the cases aforesaid, and for each such offence, over and above the damages occasioned thereby, any sum not exceeding level 1 on the standard scale* and it shall be lawful for any such churchwarden or overseer or other person as aforesaid to sell and dispose of any such manure, soil, ashes, and rubbish, or other matter or thing as aforesaid; and the proceeds arising from the sale thereof, and every such penalty as aforesaid shall, as regards any such town, or village green not awarded under the said Acts or any of them to be used as a place for exercise and recreation, be applied in aid of the rates for the repair of the public highways in the parish, and shall, as regards the land so awarded, be applied by the persons or person in whom the soil thereof may be vested in the due maintenance of such land as a place for exercise and recreation; and if any manure, soil, ashes, or rubbish be not of sufficient value to defray the expense of removing the same, the person who laid or deposited such manure, soil, ashes, or rubbish shall repay to such churchwarden or overseer or other person as aforesaid the money necessarily expended in the removal thereof; and every such penalty as aforesaid shall be recovered in manner provided by the Magistrates' Court Act 1980, and the amount of damage occasioned by any such offence as aforesaid shall, in case of dispute, be determined by the justices by whom the offender is convicted: and the payment of the amount of such damage, and the repayments of the money necessarily expended in the removal of any manure, soil, ashes, or rubbish, shall be enforced in like manner as any such penalty.

* *This amount is established by Part III of the Criminal Justice Act 1982 and may be varied by statutory instrument.*

Commons Act 1876

29. An encroachment on or inclosure of a town or village green, also any erection thereon or disturbance or interference with or occupation of the soil thereof which is made otherwise than with a view to the better enjoyment of such town or village green or recreation ground, shall be deemed to be a public nuisance, and if any person does any act in respect of which he is liable to pay damages or a penalty under section 12 of the Inclosure Act 1857, he may be summarily convicted thereof upon the information of any inhabitant of the parish in which such town or village green or recreation ground is situate, as well as upon the information of such persons as in the said section mentioned.

This section shall apply only in cases where a town or village green or recreation ground has a known and defined boundary.

Appendix 6

Scope for reform of the law on town and village greens

The present law is reasonably clear, if complex, and the procedure for new registration is reasonably satisfactory. Nonetheless there is considerable scope for improvement.

New statute

The law should be clearly and comprehensively set out in a statute. The 1965 Act is now 30 years old, and appears not to be directed towards new registration after 1990. The grounds for new registration need to be spelled out, simply, clearly and comprehensively. Common law conditions need to be replaced by statute.

Locality

The requirement for inhabitants of a defined locality is far too strict, and has defeated a number of meritorious applications. It should be made clear that use by the inhabitants of any clear administrative or geographical unit will suffice. Use by the general public should also, arguably, suffice: again, many clear examples of long use have failed to justify registration because of the predominance of 'public' users.

20 years: immediately preceding application?

Clarification is required where there has been 20 years' qualifying use but it has recently ceased, perhaps because of obstruction by the landowner. It should be confirmed that there is no requirement that the 20 years must immediately precede the application.

As of right

Reliance upon Latin tags (*nec vi, nec clam, nec precario*) should not be necessary today. Carefully drafted English is required, spelling out the objective standard required for user as of right.

Nature of the rights

The nature of the rights acknowledged by registration is unclear. They should become statutorily defined and (if they are not already) statutorily protected rights.

Structures

The nineteenth-century protective provisions should be clarified to make clear their application and scope – eg is it lawful to erect a structure such as a pavilion on a town or village green?

Dedication

There is no dedication procedure. Presumably some form of charitable trust can be set up, but even that may not make the land perpetually a green. *Oldham Borough Council* v *Attorney-General* (1993) Ch 210, CA. If the owner of entirely private land wishes to register it as a green, whether altruistically or in return for a financial grant, he should be able to, and the rights thereby created should be clear and permanent.

The regulations

The 1969 regulations are exceedingly complicated and need vigorous revision and simplification, opting for plain English wherever possible. They are in any event currently out of print, which is an unacceptable situation.

Management

Where a green has a known owner, the local authority has no statutory power of management, even in cases of default or abuse. This should be remedied.

Procedure

It is unsatisfactory that the local authority must determine applications. This involves law and evidence, and rights, and is judicial or quasi-judicial in nature. It should be handled by an independent objective lawyer sitting judicially, eg a Commons Commissioner, with a proper process set down by law.

Loss from a village green

It should be confirmed that, once registered, a town or village green is not capable of deregistration, except by Act of Parliament and, perhaps, by order of the Secretary of State. Even then there should be a requirement to substitute land which is at least equally suitable and subject to at least equally beneficial terms for the public.

Recreation allotments

It should not be lawful, if indeed it currently is, for the Charity Commissioners to make a scheme discharging a recreation allotment from the trust created by an inclosure award.

Appendix 7

Bibliography

Halsbury's Statutes, 4th edition, vol 6, reissue, 1992.

Halsbury's Laws of England, 4th edition, vol 6, reissue, 1991, pp 193-343, paras 501-800, especially para 687, pp 296-297, and paras 687-691, pp 296-300.

The Law of Commons, G D Gadsden, Sweet & Maxwell, 1988, pp 46-49, paras 2.56-2.65.

An Outline of the Law relating to Common Land and Public Access to the Countryside, B Harris and G Ryan, Sweet & Maxwell, 1967.

Our Common Right, Open Spaces Society, 1987.

Our Common Land, The Law and History of Commons and Village Greens, Paul Clayden, Open Spaces Society, 1985, reissue 1992.

A Practitioner's Guide to Common Land and the Commons Registration Act 1965, Ros Oswald, ESC Publishing, Oxford, 1989.

Making Space, Wendy Lutley, Open Spaces Society, 1992.

Report of the Royal Commission on Common Land, Cmnd 462, 1958.

Report of the Common Land Forum, Countryside Commission, 1986.

Report to Hampshire County Council in respect of Peartree Green, Southampton, by Vivian Chapman of counsel, 1992, solicitors Abels of Southampton.

Report to Berkshire County Council in respect of Emmet's Park, Binfield, Berkshire, by Vivian Chapman of counsel, 1993. Paul Clayden appeared for the applicants.

Report to Leeds City Council in respect of Post Hill Quarries, Pudsey, Leeds, West Yorkshire, by Charles George of counsel, 1988.

Registration of a new town green or village green, Alec Samuels (1992) Conveyancer 434-437 – some material from that article is used in this publication, with thanks to Messrs Sweet & Maxwell, Law Publishers.

Commons Commissioners' decisions are available from the Commons Commissioners, 4th Floor, Golden Cross House, Duncannon Street, London WC2N 4JF (0171 210 4584).